Someone
SPECIAL

Book of Quotations

D1112556

To get the full value
of joy, you must
have someone to
divide it with.
Mark Twain

The most beautiful
things in life cannot be
seen or even touched,
they must be felt
within the heart.

Helen Keller

Special people
overlook your
broken gate
and admire the
flowers in your
garden.

Where there
is great love
there are always
miracles.
Willa Cather

The future belongs
to those who believe
in the beauty of
their dreams.

Eleanor Roosevelt

11

How beautiful
the garden
whose fragrance
is family and
friends.

12

To be able to
say how much
love, is to love
but little.

Petrarch

Reach for the
moon. If you
fall short you
will land on
a star.

Harmony prevails in
the hearts of those
who are filled with
the music of love
and friendship.

16

The love of our neighbour in all its fullness simply means being able to say to him: 'What are you going through?'

Simone Weil

It's the little
blessings that
help us see, just
how lovely life
can be.

18

If you can
imagine it...
you can achieve
it. If you can
dream it... you
can become it.

A smile is
the prettiest
thing you
can wear.

Money can't buy
you love, but it
puts you in a great
bargaining position.

Little by little,
time goes by.

Short if you laugh
and long if you sigh.

If I could
choose again,
I'd still
choose you.

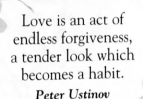

Love is an act of
endless forgiveness,
a tender look which
becomes a habit.

Peter Ustinov

Don't underestimate love at first sight. Many of us might not pass a second inspection.

27

Each day is a
gift. That's why
we call it the
present.

True love
doesn't have a
happy ending;
true love
doesn't have
an ending.

Life has taught us
that love does not
consist in gazing at
each other but in
looking outward
together in the
same direction.

Antoine de Saint-Exupery

Of all human
passions love is the
strongest, for it
attacks simultaneously
the head, the heart
and the senses.

'What are your views
on love?' 'Love?
I make it constantly
but I never talk
about it.'

Marcel Proust

33

It needs no dictionary
of quotations to
remind me that eyes
are the windows
of the soul.

Max Beerbohm

Happiness is something that comes into our lives through doors we don't even remember leaving open.

Rose Lane

To love and be loved
is to feel the sun
from both sides.

David Viscott
MD

37

...when I look on
you a moment, then
I can speak no more,
but my tongue
falls silent, and at
once a delicate
flame courses beneath

my skin, and with my
eyes I see nothing,
and my ears hum, and
a wet bathes me and
a trembling seizes
me all over...

Sappho

If you first
don't succeed in
love, try a
little ardour.

Anon

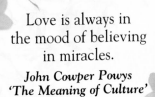

Love is always in
the mood of believing
in miracles.

John Cowper Powys
'The Meaning of Culture'

If he said quit drinking martinis, but I kept on drinking them and next morning I couldn't get out of bed, he wouldn't tell me he told me so.

Judith Viorst

43

What is lovely
never dies,

But passes into
other loveliness.

Thomas Bailey

To fear love is to
fear life, and those
who fear life are
already three
parts dead.

Bertrand Russell

Love is like quicksilver
in the hand. Leave
the fingers open
and it stays. Clutch it,
and it darts away.

Dorothy Parker

47

When one loves
somebody,
everything is
clear - where to
go, what to do
- it all takes
care of itself

and one doesn't
have to ask
anybody about
anything.

Maxim Gorky
'The Zykovs'

...she thinks me young,
Although she knows
my days are past
the best.

William Shakespeare

A difficult
achievement for
true lovers
Is to lie mute,
Without
embrace or kiss,

Without a
rustle or a
smothered sigh,
Basking in each
other's glory.

Robert Graves
'The Starred
Coverlet'

53

It's useless to try to hold people to anything they say while they're madly in love, drunk or running for office.

Love doesn't make the
world go round.
Love is what makes
the ride worthwhile.

Franklin P Jones

57

Kindness is the ability
to love people more
than they really
deserve.

Love doesn't make the
world go round.
Love is what makes
the ride worthwhile.

Franklin P Jones

Kindness is the ability
to love people more
than they really
deserve.

58

Kindness is the ability
to love people more
than they really
deserve.

Love doesn't make the
world go round.
Love is what makes
the ride worthwhile.

Franklin P Jones

57

The most lonely place
in the world is the
human heart when
love is absent.

59

Happiness is a healthy mental attitude, a grateful spirit, a clear conscience, and a heart full of love.